A GIFT OF

Miraculous Visions

FATIMA ~ CELEBRATING HER CENTENNIAL

9 8 7 6 5 4 3 2 1
Digit on right indicates the number of this printing.
Library of Congress
ISBN 978-0-615-82267-9
Photographer: Joe Roberts
Graphic Designer/Creative Consultant: Paulette Plumeri-Miller
Editors: Eric Bullard and Marcia Harriman

Printed in the United States of America
Taylor Specialty Books
Dallas, TX 75235

A GIFT OF

Miraculous Visions

FATIMA ~ CELEBRATING HER CENTENNIAL

Fatima
1917 ~ 2017

BY JOAN TARCA ALIX

Pope Francis requests his Papal Ministry be offered to Our Lady of Fatima

Most Holy Virgin,

We, the Bishops of Portugal and this multitude of pilgrims, are at Your feet in this Cova da Iria, on this 96th anniversary of Your first apparition to the Little Shepherds, in order to fulfill the desire of Pope Francis, clearly expressed, to consecrate to You, Virgin of Fatima, his Ministry of Bishop of Roma and Universal Pastor. Thus, we consecrate to You, Our Lady, You Who are the Mother of the Church, the Ministry of the new Pope; please fill his heart with the tenderness of God, which like no one else You Yourself experienced, so that he may embrace all men and women of our time with the love of Your Son Jesus Christ. Today's mankind needs to feel loved by God and by the Church. Only feeling loved she will overcome the temptation of violence, of materialism, of forgetting God, of losing the direction towards a new world, where love will reign. Please grant Pope Francis the gift of discernment in order to be able to identify the ways to renew the Church; give him courage to follow, without hesitation, the ways suggested by the Holy Spirit; support him during the difficult hours of suffering; help him overcome, in charity, the trials he'll encounter while renewing the Church. Please always be at his side, whispering to his ear those words well-known to You: *"I am the Handmaid of the Lord; be it done onto Me according to Thy Word!"*

Consecration Prayer (excerpt) by:

+ Cardinal José da Cruz Policarpo
Patriarch President of the Bishops Conference of Portugal
May 13, 2013, Fatima, Portugal

Pope Francis

Consecrates the world to the
Immaculate Heart of Mary

October 13, 2013
Saint Peter's Basilica, Vatican City

Fatima
1917 - 2017

Dedication

To my mother, Jean Lyons Tarca,
for giving me a model of faith to follow.

To my husband, Patrick Joseph Alix, and our Gifts-
Brendon, Alli, Daren, Andrea,
Kayleigh, Líadan, Emma Jean, Emiliana, and Teagan
for blessing me with infinite rewards as
your wife, mother, mother-in-law, and Méma.

Fatima
1917-2017

Contents

Introduction i

Chapter 1 ~ **Adoration** 1

Chapter 2 ~ **Offering** 11

Chapter 3 ~ **Trust** 23

Chapter 4 ~ **Love** 37

Chapter 5 ~ **Prayer** 49

Chapter 6 ~ **Celebration** 65

Chapter 7 ~ **Devotion to Our Lady** 79

Acknowledgements and Credits 97

Our Heavenly Mother appeared
in Fatima, Portugal
on the 13th day of each month from
May 13 through October 13, 1917.

Fatima
1917 ~ 2017

May 13, 2017 marks
the Centennial Anniversary of the
Apparitions of Our Lady of Fatima.

Introduction

*T*here may be no living witness today who observed the phenomenon which occurred in the tiny village of Fatima, Portugal, on October 13, 1917, but the story is well-documented. Repeated for almost a century, it tells of Mary, Mother of God, who made herself known to the world through three young Portuguese shepherd children whose lives would never be the same. For six consecutive months, Mary appeared before ultimately performing an unexplainable, heavenly miracle for tens of thousands to witness.

Her message offered the little children and rest of the world an inspirational remedy that would radically alter future events with countless miracles. Scholars agree this message applies to our world today. Fatima's story proves God's mercy bestowed upon the world through the intercession of His Blessed Mother. With this history of Fatima in mind, my commitment to Our Lady of Fatima and her message continues through creation of a celebratory centennial present: *A Gift of Miraculous Visions: Fatima~Celebrating Her Centennial.*

After reading *Fatima for Today: The Urgent Marian Message of Hope* by world-renowned Fatima authority, Father Andrew Apostoli, I became consumed with its content. I better understood Mary's message of 1917 and its application for our times. As Father Apostoli quite simply stated, her message of prayer and penance – Our Lady's remedy for peace – is more important and necessary for a world turning from God. Perhaps Our Lady's message was meant to be an ongoing call for each of us. With a second reading of Father Apostoli's book, I focused on Fatima's upcoming 2017 Centennial Celebration.

As my fascination with Fatima events evolved through research, I discovered the Sanctuary of Fatima formed a committee of scholars who in 2010 developed an academic outline in anticipation of the 2017 Fatima Centennial. The following cycles, drawn up by this council, and used for purposes of this book, represent manifestations of the 1917 Apparitions: the Events, Inspiring Sentence, Theme, Theological Nucleus, Catechetical Element, and Believing Attitude, with each aspect coinciding with a respective month of apparition.

Such meditations offer a contemporary study of scholarly text with inspirational practices such as "Pray the Rosary," "Eucharistic Adoration," "Practice of First Saturdays," and "Devotion to the Immaculate Heart of Mary." I later adapted this format of themes and cycles for each seven chapters of this book.

Through my association with the World Apostolate of Fatima Rhode Island Division, where I assisted as a volunteer, I was contacted by a Knights of Columbus member who, with his pastor, requested a First Saturday Fatima program. This experience became the catalyst for my book, *A Gift of Miraculous Visions~Fatima, Celebrating Her Centennial.* Since that time, I have met hundreds of church, school, and hospital visitors who have provided me with an opportunity for both casual and in-depth spiritual discussions.

Conversations with visitors often centered around desire for spiritual comfort, thanksgiving for blessings received, or answers to calm a doubt. My faith was truly enhanced by learning their stories. Perhaps by inspiration, I also started to realize some felt compelled to share their experiences about devotion to Mary.

I remember one woman who grew up with a grandmother who always prayed the rosary; she attributed her unwavering faith to this devotion. Another middle-aged woman had come during her lunch hour to see the pilgrim statue. Speaking in English with a slight Portuguese accent, this woman told me she grew up in the village of Fatima until age fourteen, when her family moved to the United States. With tears in her eyes, she placed a dozen white roses on the altar for her Heavenly Mother. A gentleman e-mailed his prayer petition for recovery of a nine-year old girl recently hospitalized with an aggressive cancer. His heartfelt plea spoke to his belief, reading in part, "*I know Our Lady hears all prayers, especially those for children.*"

I recorded copious notes of these visitor stories. Their worthy accounts were such an inspiration to me, I felt they should be shared. Then, I asked school-age children to give their thoughts to the Fatima phrases contained within each chapter.

To that end, at the conclusion of each chapter I included thoughts of children and vignettes to enlighten the reader. Collectively, comments by the children and visitors offer a chance to join others as witnesses to the Fatima message of today.

Whether reading a hard-cover edition or online format of *A Gift of Miraculous Visions: Fatima~Celebrating Her Centennial*, my hope is to inspire emulation of devotional practices shown to the children of Fatima in 1917. From their personal encounters and memoirs, along with accounts of over 70,000 pilgrims who witnessed the promised miracle, these perceptions of Mary enable us to believe.

As we look forward to Fatima's Centennial Celebration of 2017, may we bring Our Lady's proven remedy of prayer and penance to everyone living today.

Joan M. Alix

Joan Tarca Alix

Fatima
1917~2017

Adoration

*I*n the spring of 1916, three shepherd children tended daily to their flock of sheep. **Lucia Dos Santos**, age ten, and her two cousins, **Jacinta** and **Francisco Marto**, ages seven and nine, encountered an Angel. This Angel appeared to the children on three separate occasions and prepared them with an awe and splendor for what they would later witness.

As reported by Lucia many years later, during each Angel visit an unexplained intensity of God would envelope them.

Fatima
1917 - 2017

My God I Believe

Most
Holy Trinity
I adore You
Profoundly

The One and Triune God

Trinitarian Face of God

A Child's Thoughts on Adoration

"Always be ready; God has different ways and times to express His love." ~ Dakota, age 12

"Adoration means singing to Him." ~ David, age 7

"Angels give messages. We receive the message and bring it completely back to God." ~ Ricardo, age 12

"Preparation for sheer beauty." ~ Jack, age 12

"Angels adore God by obeying Him." ~ Emma, age 8

"Adoration means caring." ~ Mikajla, age 7

"Singing to Him is Adoration." ~ David, age 7

Adoration as the Angel of Fatima Taught Us

*F*ew individuals can boast of dedicating their life for children with the same sort of passion and zeal as shown by **Susan Rizzo Vincent**. When she lost her only child, a twenty-four year-old, to a drunk driver, Susan created a program to provide dance therapy for children diagnosed with cancer. Her efforts seemingly defy normal human explanation.

After months of utter despair and hopelessness, Susan initiated a foundation to help others in her daughter's memory. Now, ten years later, Susan continues to plan, organize and speak at events nationwide to offer children with cancer an outlet through dance therapy.

Most people are unaware Susan's strength is derived from her weekly hour of Eucharistic Adoration. Here in the Real Presence, Susan often ponders the mysteries of the Rosary. This meditative time affords Susan a deep and everlasting comfort. She has found this practice helps her to listen with her heart to His message for her. And, through the Rosary, Susan connects with her heavenly mother. Sometimes an idea will be solidified; sometimes an answer will become clear. Susan confides, *"I still wonder and question, but I find a sense of peace by my silent devotional practice in the Real Presence."*

Read more about Susan and her work at **www.DreasDream.org**.

Offering of Oneself

May 1917 Apparition

A Lady of **indescribable beauty** appeared to the little shepherds Jacinta, Francisco and their cousin, Lucia. The Beautiful Lady asked the children to return on the 13th day for six consecutive months. She promised to reveal her true identity and told them to pray. This unexpected sighting compelled the three children to offer daily sacrifices to God.

Fatima
1917 - 2017

Do you want to offer yourselves to God?

God the Savior

Sharers in
the Redemption

A Child's Thoughts on Offering of Oneself

"Only children can see the true power of God and the saints." ~ Edward, age 12

"They must have believed with all of their hearts to have seen Our Lady!" ~ Eva, age 12

"The Lovely Rose, Mary." ~ Olivia, age 12

"Prayer helps us to talk with God. It may not happen face-to-face but through grace of the Holy Spirit." ~ Will, age 12

"Any age can follow God's will. All you have to do is pray." ~ Kylee, age 12

"We can use up all of our play time and say a Hail Mary to give to God." ~ Jayden, age 7

Offering of Oneself

*I*magine being told you have six months to live. **Judy Studer** was given this prognosis. She had already experienced the loss of both a daughter and a grandson. At the same time, her five-year old granddaughter Jessica had been diagnosed with a childhood cancer. Judy's world came to a sudden halt. But intuitively, her work as a hospital nurse qualified her to never question a medical diagnosis. However, the doctor's advice to Judy, *"Prepare yourself. You have about six months to live,"* was totally unexpected.

Readying her family for her final days, Judy accepted what God had given her. Her elderly mother who was also Jessica's great-grandmother, told Judy to pray to Mother Mary. Judy replied, *"Mom, I'm a nurse. I know about these things, and my doctor says it's too late for me."*

Judy's mother pointed her finger boldly in her daughter's face and told her, *"You may be too old to listen to me, but you're not to old to pray to your heavenly mother."* So, in respect to her mother's simple request, Judy began to pray to Mary for the will of her Son.

As cancer treatments continued, a call from her doctor's office urged Judy to come in and bring her husband. Judy sensed the end was near. However, her doctor explained the cancer covering over fifty percent of Judy's body had disappeared—the likes of which he rarely had seen. Judy screamed, *"It's Our Lady, Our Lady."*

Eventually, Judy returned to her work as a nurse, never forgetting a prayer-promise she had made to God. Meanwhile, Judy's only granddaughter Jessica who was now thirteen years old, showed signs of remission. Family prayer now included a daily thanksgiving to God for their numerous blessings.

Through spiritual guidance, Judy became an active member of a local division of the World Apostolate of Fatima (WAF). Then she became custodian and guardian of a Fatima Pilgrim Statue for the WAF USA. Presently, over ten years later, Judy accepts her responsibility and travels the world as an ambassador for Our Lady of Fatima. She has visited Ireland, India, Portugal, and Italy, as well as numerous Dioceses throughout the United Sates.

Several years ago while visiting Portugal, the late Father Kondor, former Postulator for the canonization of Jacinta and Francisco, presented Judy with first-class relics of the two little shepherd children, telling her, *"I ask you to offer these relics for veneration to others, especially the young people of the world. May these bring comfort and healing while you travel with the icon of Our Lady sharing her message."*

Recently, Jessica, a nineteen-year old college student, was awarded Miss Rhode Island 2013. She impressed the judges with her strong faith-filled convictions and creative volunteer service program for children. While being crowned with this honor, it came as no surprise to many audience members that Jessica raised both hands upward immediately thanking, "God and His Mother."

Both grandmother and granddaughter have unselfishly volunteered countless hours bringing Our Lady's message of prayer to others. Even today, Jessica often accompanies her grandmother to school and church visits. In all of their roles, both Judy and Jessica attempt to embody the delivered message of Our Lady telling of Mary's promise.

Today, as a wife, mother of three, grandmother of three, oncology nurse at a Rhode Island hospital, traveler, spokesperson, and custodian for the United Nations International Pilgrim of the World Apostolate of Fatima USA, Judy continues her many called vocations. In Judy Studer's own words, *"One of my most important vocations allows me to help others realize the love of Our Lady and mercy of her Son."*

CHAPTER THREE

Trust

June 1917 Apparition

*W*hen the Beautiful Lady appeared on the 13th day of June, the three Little Shepherds became mystified by her splendor. As they became enthralled in her indescribable rapture, the children petitioned the Lady to take them with her. It was during this apparition that the three children experienced an aura of heaven.

"We saw ourselves in this immense light, as it were, immersed in God."

- Quote from IV Memoir of Sister Lucia written in 1941

Fatima
1917-2017

My Immaculate Heart shall be your refuge and a way to leading you to God

Do not be afraid

The God of the Promise

TRUST

Christian Hope

A Child's Thoughts on Trust

"I know Mary loves me." ~ Kaleigh Rae, age 5

"Trust God always and everywhere." ~ Matthew, age 12

"Enlightenment at its finest!" ~ Erik, age 12

"Never lose hope." ~ Celine, age 12

"Mary is completely pure and enthralling; mortals could barely contain her beauty." ~ Jack, age 12

"Trusting in Jesus." ~ Adam, age 7

"Ask and you shall receive." ~ Luke, age 12

"Never be afraid to ask God for trust." ~ Adam, age 12

Trust

$\mathcal{A}$ll airlines require an extensive security baggage search prior to the United Nations Pilgrim Statue being brought on board. The custodian of this icon removes it from a custom golf bag and fastens it to an assigned front window seat on the airplane. Despite the statue being over sixty-five years old, a full-price ticket is paid with no senior discount applied.

It is not uncommon for airplane boarders to stop, inquire, and wonder in amazement at the Heavenly Mother belted in place. Believers and non-believers alike inevitably seem to comment about how much safer they feel with Mary on board their flight.

Once all passengers are seated and secured, the airplane takes off for its destination. Airline attendants always want to hear about the story of Fatima. Typically, they somehow manage to overlook people who are standing and kneeling in the front aisle listening to the custodian's account. Several passengers lean and stretch forward, trying to hear every word spoken by the statue custodian. All continues smoothly while the airplane is 33,000 feet in the air. No one questions who is in control.

On one such recent flight, a woman approaches the custodian who is reverently showing something to other passengers.

"Could you show that to me, and is it magic?" she asks.

While holding the carefully preserved remains for veneration of Jacinta and Francisco, the custodian replies, *"These are first-class relics. They are not magic; it represents faith."* The inquisitive passenger loudly announces to other passengers that she was born and raised a Catholic, and just wants to know more. Although she has heard of Fatima in the past, her interest is now piqued, and now wants to know everything about Our Lady of Fatima. As she returns to her seat, she lets others know she wants to come back to the church.

While in flight, a young gentleman who was seated in back of the plane comes forward to visit the custodian. He explains his wife is Catholic, but he is not, and that his 38 year-old wife has lung cancer despite having never smoked. Together, they are traveling to enable her to receive extensive chemotherapy treatments. He kindly asks the custodian to pray for his wife who is unable to get a closer look at the statue. The custodian gets up and visits with the woman. Together they pray. The woman cries as the custodian offers her a gift rosary from Fatima. The wife says she feels something special. Departing from the plane, the husband stops and says to the custodian that he could sense his wife's new-found peace. Now, as a result, he truly wants to explore becoming a Catholic.

Yet another passenger's account involves two separate meetings with the statue: one on the plane and the other several days later. "When I boarded the plane from Chicago to California, I noticed a woman carrying a golf bag onto the airplane. Upon exiting, I caught a glimpse of a beautiful statue. The woman next to the statue, its custodian, offered me and all exiting passengers a bookmark printed with Angel of Portugal prayers, website and e-mail address. I stuffed it into my bag and thought nothing of it."

"Several days and numerous business meetings later, I returned to my hotel room. I emptied my purse and the bookmark caught my attention. I googled the website and statue's scheduled itinerary. Could it be possible this beautiful image would still be in California and only blocks from my hotel? The next morning I took a cab to the indicated church. I spoke briefly with the custodian and she remembered me from the plane. I was then able to pray in the Presence of Jesus and the image of His Holy Mother! These unexpected visits turned into a miracle for me!"

Upon landing, both flight attendants express an interest in having the statue visit their home states. Both take pictures with their phones. One attendant sends the photo to her Facebook page and gets several immediate responses. Our Lady of Fatima reaches the internet world before she is even removed from her seat!

For security reasons, the statue is always the last to be removed from the airplane. However, on one particular flight, the pilot comes out to visit the statue and takes his photo with this beautiful image to send to his wife and children. The pilot becomes so intrigued with the statue and her travels, he offers to help the custodian. He insists on carrying the statue off of the airplane and up the ramp to the gate, as he *"wants the privilege of carrying my Holy Mother off the plane."* For him, this simple act of grace represents an enormous honor.

CHAPTER FOUR

Love

July 1917 Apparition

During this third encounter on July 13th, the Beautiful Lady requested prayer and penance in honor of Our Lady of the Rosary. A frightening vision was presented to the children. Although this proved the reality of hell, the Lady offered a consoling remedy for world peace if her message was heeded. She told the children in the end, her **Immaculate Heart** would triumph.

Fatima
1917-2017

*Oh Jesus,
it is for
the love of You*

*Enveloped
in the love of God
for the world*

The Compassionate God

The Love that purifies and saves

A Child's Thoughts on Love

"Love is all you need." ~ Josh, age 12

"Love cannot be broken." ~ Austin, age 12

"Our Holy Mother is most compassionate." ~ Celine age 12

"If the world listens, we will hear the secrets of heaven." ~ Ashley, age 12

"Be loving." ~ Dakota, age 12

"In the end, God will conquer all evil." ~ Cade, age 12

"Love is my mom and dad." ~ David, age 7

Love

"My entry into the church was prompted by a profound experience in 1946 in Panama City when I returned from duty in Japan with the U.S. Navy. While there on leave, my best friend – a Catholic – and I decided to visit a famous landmark, Saint Joseph Church. It was the first time I ever entered a Catholic church. When I walked toward the sanctuary, I was stunned to silence and overwhelmed with awe by what had to be the unmistakable Presence of God. Why He chose me is still a mystery, but I have always been grateful He did. I soon recovered, and I don't think my friend was aware of my spiritual transformation. This experience at Saint Joseph Church in Panama City was a first, but not a last.

"In 1949, I returned and settled in my hometown. About a year later while walking along Main Street, I recognized a girl, named Lori, standing alongside her mother. I vividly recalled that prior to my military assignment, this girl and I had a mutual group of friends. I stopped to say hello and reintroduce myself to both her and her mother. I realized I felt a strong attraction to Lori, and decided to pursue her friendship. The next day, I phoned Lori and we talked for hours. We discovered our feelings were mutual. And, she was Catholic. This was problematic because my family had no tolerance for religion – especially Catholicism.

"We began dating and I asked Lori to introduce me to a Catholic priest. She knew nothing about my spiritual awakening in Panama City. But I wanted to become a Catholic and asked for her help. Initially doubting my sincerity, Lori eventually introduced me to a priest, who through instruction, baptized me into the Catholic faith.

"Lori and I married, and our love for each other was entwined with devotion to Mary. I intuitively felt Lori was someone God had chosen for me to be my wife. During our years with the World Apostolate of Fatima (WAF), we worked together to spread devotional practices and plan events. We were always open to challenges and our responses to Mary were always, 'Here we are, use us.' And, on many occasions Our Lady did.

"During one particular month-long pilgrim visit in our diocese, it seemed no parish wanted to host the statue on Easter Sunday. We worried that Our Lady would be forgotten until at the last minute a call came from a Vietnamese church whose parishioners pleaded for an Easter Sunday visit. This event was featured in an issue of *Soul* magazine entitled, 'The Day No One Wanted Our Lady.'

"So many happenings in my life could be considered amazing, I often wonder how I can repay God and His Blessed Mother for the numerous graces received, fully realizing this is impossible. Lori had to be a gift from God especially to get me into the Church. She was a most wonderful wife. We truly loved each other for sixty-three years and we were married over fifty-eight years before her death last year.

"I believe God sends His love to us through the hands of His Mother and the love I return to Him goes through those hands as well."

~ *R.A.R., age 85*

CHAPTER 5

Prayer

August 1917 Apparition

This time the Beautiful Lady's words contained a request for continued **prayers and sacrifices**. She reaffirmed her desire for the world to offer reparation for others through **prayer**.

Fatima
1917~2017

Pray, pray much and make sacrifices for sinners

Sanctified in Christ

Holy God

The Church as the Communion of Saints

A Child's Thoughts on Prayer

"Praying will help you in the hardest of times." ~ Edward, age 12

*"Our Lady wants people to pray more to make the world
a better place."* ~ Jack, age 12

"Praying forms a clearer path to heaven!" ~ Olivia, age 12

"Praying is singing to Jesus." ~ Sophia, age 7

"God will always forgive us as long as we pray." ~ Dakota, age 12

"Sacrifice is prayer to God." ~ Elena, age 12

"Pray now and always." ~ Celine, age 12

"Pray for those less fortunate." ~ Dylan, age 7

"Praying is saying words that show you care for people."
~ Matthew, age 7

Power of Prayer

*W*hile browsing in a small museum in the village of Aljustrel, Portugal, where the well-known shepherds had lived, I met a shopkeeper introducing herself as Guilhermena Vieira Rosa Santos Silva, who spoke and understood some English. Guilma, as she is called, related her family connection to Lucia, the eldest visionary. She humbly stated that her mother-in-law, Maria dos Anjos (Maria of the Angels) is daughter to Lucia's oldest sister. Both Guilma, age sixty-two, and Maria dos Anjos, age ninety-three, have lived their entire lives in the famous village. As our talk continued, Guilma offered to introduce me to her mother-in-law.

On the next afternoon, while we were walking to her mother-in-law's home, Guilma began to talk about her favorite book and movie: *The Life of John Paul II* and *The Passion of Christ*. Guilma is a mother of three sons and works five days a week as the sole docent in the museum, a replica of an early 1900's Portuguese home.

Seven days a week, having never missed a day, Guilma goes to the famous Shrine. These visits are perhaps what define her. "I feel it is a privilege and honor to live here. I must go to the chapel daily to pray for all pilgrims and visitors."

As our conversation continued, Guilma proudly stated, "Author John de Marchi, who wrote *Fatima from the Beginning*, interviewed my grandfather about what he witnessed on the day of the Miracle. When I was a little girl, my grandfather told me how the sun danced and danced! He would say he could not imagine this Miracle as anything but the Hand of God, touching the earth."

Guilma then shared a family story with me. "In Coimbra, next to the Carmelite Convent where Sister Lucia lived until her death in 2005 at age ninety-eight, is a hospital with many reported miracles. In 1980, I was taken the distance by ambulance to this same hospital to have our first child, a son. Days later, my husband, mother-in-law, and father-in-law, came to get me and our baby to return to our village. On February 13th, we all left the hospital by taxi and to my surprise, we went directly to the Coimbra convent. We visited with Sister Lucia, who was thrilled to see the newest member of our family. Sister Lucia gave me a hand-embroidered gift she had made for our first-born son. I still have this present."

While focusing on her personal relationship with Lucia, Guilma added, "At the Carmelite Convent in Coimbra, I would ask Mother Superior to allow a visit with Lucia. Even though we were concealed by a cloister grate, I would speak to Lucia about my own struggles and challenges. Often, my mother-in-law would accompany me to the Convent.

"We traveled back four or five times a year and as well as every holiday to visit with Sister Lucia, who would talk continuously and ask about family members. Lucia was happy, but at times she became saddened by world events. Sister Lucia reminded us to do as Our Lady asked to make our world a better place.

"Being alone with Lucia was so special for me. Lucia was my best friend. Often, she would talk with me, like I was her best friend.

"I've learned it is important for us to be in communion with Our Lady and her Son. This union becomes intensified for me. Now, when I have problems, I go to Our Lady. I speak to her. I feel her help. To live close to where Our Lady appeared reaffirms my faith."

Then, we approached the home of Guilma's mother-in-law, another favored relative of Lucia. Wearing black, a Portuguese custom for mourning her husband's death, Maria dos Angos, Lucia's niece, prays the Rosary each day on the exact place where the Angel appeared in 1916 to the three children. With rosary in hand, Maria, began her proud testimony with a smile.

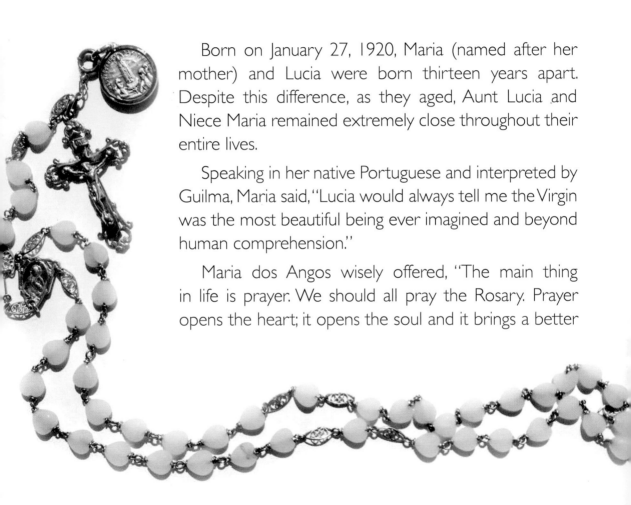

Born on January 27, 1920, Maria (named after her mother) and Lucia were born thirteen years apart. Despite this difference, as they aged, Aunt Lucia and Niece Maria remained extremely close throughout their entire lives.

Speaking in her native Portuguese and interpreted by Guilma, Maria said, "Lucia would always tell me the Virgin was the most beautiful being ever imagined and beyond human comprehension."

Maria dos Angos wisely offered, "The main thing in life is prayer. We should all pray the Rosary. Prayer opens the heart; it opens the soul and it brings a better world. This is the most precious connection to heaven." With profound wisdom, Maria dos Angos concluded, "Even today, both young and old must remember the Virgin speaks to her children through prayer. Lucia was a perfect example of this.

"People must do what God asks, but be good to others – as a sister with her brother or a husband with his wife. We must look inside of ourselves to better know others. Only then will we understand others. As Lucia said, 'Look at the other person like you are looking at yourself.'"

Quite unexpectedly, a chance stop at a small village museum led to a special visit with two remarkable women who willingly shared personal and treasured memories of their beloved relative, Lucia. More importantly, the daily devotions of Guilma and Maria dos Anjos can serve as models for pilgrims everywhere.

Celebration

September 1917 Apparition

By this time, thousands of pilgrims and curiosity seekers gathered in the Cova of Fatima. As a result, the three children now held numerous prayer requests close to their hearts given to them by the crowds.

When the Lady arrived on the **13th of September**, she continued to ask for sacrifices and prayers for peace. Our Lady reminded the children of her promise to perform a **Miracle** in October for all to see.

Fatima
1917 - 2017

God is pleased with your Sacrifices

I came that they might have Life

God, the fullness of Life

*Sharing
in the abundant
Life of God*

A Child's Thoughts on Celebration

"Celebration is the miracle of Mary." ~ Dylan, age 7

"God asks only small things from us, but they add up." ~ Devin, age 12

"Be faithful! Be humble, for you only have one God!" ~ Erik, age 12

"Never ever lose faith in God." ~ Lindsay, age 12

"We celebrate when we sing to God." ~ Natalie, age 7

God will always keep His promise with us and celebrate."
~ Elena, age 7

"We can celebrate in all things by staying closer through prayer."
~ Matthew, age 12

A Parish Celebration

The following letter of thanks was shared on behalf of all who organized a Saturday parish event in which over 350 participants attended a Mass and First Saturday Devotional Practices.

Dear Father Malley,

I wish to thank you for your blessings, leadership and support of this past weekend's event with the United Nations Pilgrim Statue of Our Lady of Fatima.

You embraced the idea of having Our Lady of Fatima visit the Parish for an entire day encompassing Adoration, Praying of the Rosary, two Masses and even personally chanting the Chaplet of Divine Mercy. The traditions of our parish were displayed throughout the day and Benediction with Fr. Sojan was special. The Music Ministry transformed us with their selections. We were all filled with awe in the presence of Our Lady of Fatima.

Brother Andres Juarez, Knights of Columbus, brought the message of Our Lady of Fatima to our parish early on in the year and our former pastor accepted pending your arrival. I thank Andres, his wife, Janie and son, Daniel for their support and hosting of coordination meetings in their home.

I wish to thank Cindy Vinal for her assistance in coordinating the event ensuring all support was available and also for being a witness in Prayer during the day. The Dominicans bless the roses and say that "the rose is a perfect figure of the excellence of the Holy Rosary, and of its different mysteries." There is no coincidence, and for this I thank Connie Sanchez and Stella Mazer for their gift of four dozen white roses offered to Our Lady of Fatima and whose color White represents The Joyful Mysteries.

To our Grand Knight Joe Gengo and the support of the Honor Guard headed by our District Deputy and Honor Guard Commander, Walt Atzert, thank you for keeping the faith with our own council. Our Knights of Columbus witnessed an event that strengthened our Faith knowing that we are consecrated to the Blessed Virgin Mary.

To Judith Studer: You were sent here through the intercession of our Mother and were a ray of sunshine and support in resources and prayer.

Throughout the past months, your ministry and its blessings were passed on to many within our St. Timothy parish and other parishes within this Diocese.

Finally, to the hundreds of men, women and children from St. Timothy and surrounding parishes of our Diocese. Thank you for your participation and for the prayers offered and those requested from our Mother. The Holy Spirit was present in his work through the faithful.

This could not have been accomplished without the hand of God orchestrating us all. God Bless!

Eric E. Matos
Dr. Gilbert Ortiz Council #13525, Knights of Columbus
St. Timothy Catholic Church
Lutz, FL

CHAPTER 7

Devotion to Our Lady

October 1917 Apparition

*T*orrential rains began on October 12th and continued on October 13th as crowds numbering 70,000 or so gathered. Then at the prescribed hour, the rains stopped and all clothing quickly became dried.

The **phenomenon of the sun**, witnessed by thousands of spectators, initially frightened the crowd with its intensity. The sun trembled, made sudden movements beyond all cosmic law and "danced" according to testimonies later given by witnesses. Vivid colors appeared to reflect on the entirety of the crowds.

Fatima
1917-2017

According to the ***IV Memoir of Sister Lucia***, Our Lady said to the children, ***"I want to tell you that a chapel is to be built here in my honor. I am the Lady of the Rosary. Continue to pray the Rosary every day."*** Then, distinct visions of Our Lady, Saint Joseph and the Child Jesus were bequeathed to Lucia, Jacinta and Francisco.

When the sun returned to normal, there was an explosion of joy. The dancing of the sun was enough to convince every spectator that Our Lady's appearances were truly the hands of God. Everyone joined in thanksgiving and praise for Our Lady, Mother of God.

I am the Lady of the Rosary

The Lord did great things

The God of the Covenant

Mary in Salvation History

A Child's Thoughts on Devotion to Our Lady

"She is the Mother of God and she protects me."
~ Sofía Marie, age 6

*"The Miracle of Fatima makes me believe and
love God all the more."* ~ Lindsay, age 12

"Anything is possible with the Rosary." ~ Ricardo, age 12

"Spectacular!" ~ John, age 7

*"Mary was completely pure and enthralling; mortals could
barely contain Her beauty."* ~ Tony, age 12

*"When I'm feeling down, she gives me a kind of inner
strength I can't describe."* ~ Samuel Raymond, age 16

Devotion to Our Lady

"*D*espite being in my forties, I have truly become a changed man. Until a few weeks ago, I had no interest in church. I even told my own mother that she was wasting her time going to daily Mass and church was a joke. Don't get me wrong, something in my life was missing but I just didn't know what. Then, through a set of remarkable coincidences, I was able to finally find my faith by virtue of my discovery of the Fatima story.

"Three months ago, my wife had connected on Facebook with an uncle, a doctor living in Spain, who has a great devotion to Our Lady of Fatima. So much so, he even named his first-born daughter, Fatima, in her honor. Additionally, I learned my wife's birthday was the same day as a significant Fatima celebration – May 13th.

"I wondered if these Fatima connections were merely coincidental so I began to research this story. After reading numerous accounts of the children and Miracle of the Sun, I became consumed with Fatima events.

"While I couldn't believe so many years passed by before I discovered this miraculous story, it slowly began to change my perspective on church. We started to attend Sunday Mass for the first time as a family. By our third Sunday Mass, a record for us, my wife showed me the bulletin promoting a Fatima presentation. This time, we both thought this was more than coincidence.

"On Saturday afternoon, the day of the Fatima event, our children were as demanding as ever. However, my wife encouraged me to attend if only for a short visit.

"Quickly, I went to church thinking I'd only stay for fifteen minutes. First, I felt the need to case things out so I'd be comfortable being at church, especially on a Saturday. All of this was so new to me. As I walked toward the front altar, I felt guided by the Host of Jesus on the main altar. Off to the side, I saw a beautiful statue of Our Lady of Fatima adorned with roses. Instantly, I felt overwhelmed but sensed an inner calmness.

"After some quiet prayer time, I met the custodian of the statue. She showed me relics, told me of their significance, and explained how to venerate these special treasures. I remember her saying that it would be the same as if Jacinta and Francisco were actually here praying with me.

"I began to pray to Saint Joseph for help as a father and husband. I continued to feel completely in awe and sensed a heavenly splendor. Actually, I couldn't believe what had just happened. I became spellbound. I had come to church merely out of sheer curiosity but I found myself instead at the beginning of a pilgrimage. How could I explain all of these Our Lady of Fatima coincidences?

"As I began to leave the church, I saw a priest. We said hello and I casually mentioned that one of these days I'd like to get together with him for a talk. 'Well,' he replied, 'how about right now?' It was then I went to confession for the first time in over twelve years. I left church on that Saturday feeling transformed.

"The next day I received the Eucharist at Sunday Mass. My life today includes daily prayer and devotions. The story of Our Lady and the message of Fatima changed my life. And would you believe just like my mother, I now attend daily Mass."

~ B.F., age 44

SONG OF

Our Lady of Fatima

BY GLADYS GOLLAHON

Ave Maria Ave Maria
The heavens were opened Our Lady appeared at Fatima one day
To tell us again of the great need for prayer
As Her children we answer this way.

REFRAIN
Dear Lady of Fatima we come on bended knee
To beg your intercession for peace and unity.
Dear Mary won't you show us, the right and shining way
We pledge our love and offer you a Rosary each day.

You promised at Fatima each time that you appeared
To help us if we pray to you to banish war and fear
Dear Lady on first Saturdays we ask your guiding hand
For grace and guidance here on earth and protection for our land.

In 1950, Gladys Gollahon (1908-1996), a 42-year-old Ohio homemaker, wife of a bus driver, and mother of three children, wrote the song 'Our Lady of Fatima', as a result of her own prayers for peace. Later, Gladys spent $2.50 and had her song recorded. She never expected that her tribute to Our Lady would become a top musical hit and performed by famed celebrities for years to come.

May the words of Gladys Gollahon convey a celebratory Centennial gift of prayer and accurate practice for all the faithful in following the Message of Our Lady of Fatima.

*"The Rosary is my favorite prayer.
To pray the Rosary is to hand over our burdens to the merciful Hearts of Christ and His Mother."*
~ **Blessed Pope John Paul II**

"The Most Holy Virgin in these last times in which we live has given a new efficacy to the recitation of the Rosary to such an extent that there is no problem, no matter how difficult it is, whether temporal or above all spiritual, in the personal life of each one of us, of our families...that cannot be solved by the Rosary. There is no problem, I tell you, no matter how difficult it is, that we cannot resolve by the prayer of the Holy Rosary."
~ **Sister Lucia dos Santos, Fatima Visionary**

"One day, through the Rosary, Our Lady will save the world."
~ **Saint Dominic**

Constantly holding a Rosary, even while working, she said, "It's like holding hands with Our Lady in whom I place my trust."
~ **Mother Theresa of Calcutta**

Acknowledgments and Credits

A Gift of Miraculous Visions: Fatima~Celebrating Her Centennial began through a series of coincidental meetings. First I found a skilled photographer, **Joe Roberts**. His artistic ability captured and blended with each written contemplative as developed by the Sanctuary of Fatima 2017 Centennial Committee. His passionate style, and devout faith, bring a colorful visual for practicing Our Lady of Fatima's modern promise. I am most sincerely grateful for Joe Roberts' giftedness.

As I continued to write, a personal connection to the three shepherd children to today's children seemed necessary. **Ms. Carmen Ruelf**, teacher at Most Holy Redeemer School in Tampa, Fl , shared with her students the Fatima story and Centennial outline. She then asked her students to meditate and freely respond to the words and phrases of each chapter. These humble tributes of the children serve to encourage prayerful thoughts from present-day readers. To Ms. Ruelf and her students, I thank you for believing in miracles and for your devotion to Our Lady.

With a structural plan in place, my project continued. I visited Fatima, Portugal, and met with **Sister Angela Coelho**, religious member of the Alliance of Holy Mary, Professor, Medical Doctor, and Vice-Postulator for the Canonization of Francisco and Jacinta. Sister Coelho served on the prestigious Sanctuary of Fatima Committee that developed the Centennial Itinerary. I shared my book idea with her and sought her guidance in requesting permission to use the 2017 outline.

Upon my return home, I received permission from **Father Carlos Cabecinhas**, Rector of the Sanctuary of Fatima, to use the Centennial documents and outline. I am sincerely indebted to Sister Angela Coelho and Father Carlos Cabecinhas for their supportive roles in my work and their embodiment of Our Lady's Centennial message.

After hearing about this project, **Paulette Plumeri-Miller** became a trusted and dedicated supporter. She offered unparalleled talent and acclaimed skills. Paulette, an award-winning graphic designer and creative artistic consultant, made the difference by incorporating her gifts as a work of prayer.

There are still so many individuals who must be recognized:

- **Father Andrew Apostoli, Father Robert Bailey**, Father Paul **Desmarais, Father Matt Mauriello, Father Kenneth Malley, Father Len Piotrowski**, and **Father Albert Shuyaka**.

- **Ana Reis** and **Nuno Prazeres**, International Secretariats of the World Apostolate of Fatima (WAF)-Portugal, and **Deacon Bob Ellis**, National Director of the WAF USA-New Jersey.

- **Joe Gengo, Eric** and **Margarita Matos, Andres** and **Jane Juarez, John Kane, Mary Scott, Vicky Hite, Ed** and **Susan Bilbao**.

- **Eric Bullard, Marcia Harriman, Crystal Weary**, and **Susan Rizzo Vincent**.

- And love to my brothers **Fred, Paul**, and **Dan Tarca, sisters** and **brothers-in-law, nieces** and **nephews**.

Finally, to the **visitors** who daily practice Our Lady's Fatima message in their parishes, this account would not be possible without your willingness to share your journey.

Photo Locations and Credits

Photographer Joe Roberts utilized the following locations to offer a glimpse of the contemporary message of Fatima:

- **Bethany Center** - Saint Petersburg Diocese, Lutz, FL
- **Christ the King Catholic Church,** Tampa, FL
- **Espiritu Santo Catholic Church,** Safety Harbor, FL
- **Holy Family Catholic Church**, Saint Petersburg, FL
- **Incarnation Catholic Church,** Tampa, FL
- **Our Lady of Divine Providence House of Prayer,** Clearwater, FL
- **Sacred Heart Catholic Church,** Tampa, FL
- **Saint Paul's Catholic Church,** Tampa, FL
- **Saint Timothy Catholic Church,** Lutz, FL
- **Santo Nino National Shrine** - Saint Petersburg Diocese, Tampa, FL

Page 27 photo by **Jason Siegel** of FOCUS Seek 2013, Orlando, FL

Page 78 photo by **Paulette Plumeri-Miller**, Tampa, FL

Page 88 photo by **Neil Rausbaum**, Immaculate Conception Catholic Church, Jacksonville, FL

MY WISH IS TO OFFER THIS **LOGOTYPE** AS A GIFT TO DEVOTED **FATIMA FOLLOWERS** TO HELP BRAND THIS REMARKABLE MILESTONE EVENT. THE GRACEFUL, FLOWING SCRIPT FONT WAS CHOSEN TO REPRESENT THE **HEAVENLY APPARITIONS** AND A CONNECTION TO OUR EARTHLY WORLD. THE DATES MARK THE **100-YEAR** TIMESPAN FROM THE FIRST **APPARITION** TO THE UPCOMING **CENTENNIAL** CELEBRATION YEAR. FLOURISHES FROM THE CAPITAL LETTER "F" HELP CREATE THE APPEARANCE OF RIBBON, TIED TOGETHER TO FORM A BOW, REPRESENTING **OUR LADY OF FATIMA'S GIFT** TO THE **THREE SHEPHERDS** OF THEN, AND THE **PEOPLE OF THE WORLD** TODAY.

~Paulette Plumeri-Miller
Graphic Designer/Creative Consultant
Tampa, Florida

About the Designer

When asked to become an integral part of the development of this book, **Paulette Plumeri-Miller** enthusiastically embraced the challenge, responding without hesitation. Her devotion to Mary began as a child. After mass on Sunday, she would often visit the Basilica of the National Shrine of Our Lady of Fatima with her family, located in Lewiston, NY, near Niagara Falls. Those were very special memories.

Upon graduating from State University of New York at Buffalo with a Bachelor of Fine Arts degree in Visual Communications, Paulette began freelance work and later relocated from her hometown of Niagara Falls to Tampa, FL.

Paulette currently resides in Tampa with her husband, Corky, and son, Sam, where she is a full-time graphic designer, art director and creative consultant.

About the Photographer

After graduating from the University of South Florida with a degree in photography, **Joe Roberts** launched Roberts Imagery, a company providing photography for celebratory events. His experience throughout the USA and Europe expanded his knowledge of photographic documentation to tell a story. Joe's skills and talents abound in this book to Our Lady of Fatima. Joe Roberts currently resides in Tampa, FL, where he specializes in professional wedding photography.

Please visit Joe at www.robertsimagery.com.

About the Author

Joan Tarca Alix's motto of Faith~Family~Friends inspired the creation of *A Gift of Miraculous Visions: Fatima~Celebrating Her Centennial*. Members of Espiritu Santo Church, Saint Petersburg Diocese, Joan and her husband, Patrick, reside in Tampa, FL, where many components of this book developed. Joan is most grateful for the support shown by her treasured family and friends.

You may email Joan at Joan@FatimaGiftBook2017.com
For additional copies or to become a GIFT SPONSOR, please visit
www.FatimaGiftBook2017.com

Fatima
1917 - 2017